**Play** Foundations

# My Friends and Me

**Jenni Tavener**

# Acknowledgements

© 2008 Folens Limited, on behalf of the author.

United Kingdom: Folens Publishers, Waterslade House, Thame Road, Haddenham, Buckinghamshire HP17 8NT.

Email: folens@folens.com

Ireland: Folens Publishers, Greenhills Road, Tallaght, Dublin 24.

Email: info@folens.ie

Commissioning editor: Zoë Nichols

Managing editor: Jane Morgan        Editor: Jane Bishop

Design and layout: Infuze Ltd        Illustrations: Gaynor Berry

Cover design: Infuze Ltd        Cover illustration: Cathy Hughes

With thanks to the following for their permission to use extracts:

All Early learning goals and Aspects of learning quoted in this book are taken from *Practice Guidance for the Early Years Foundation Stage* (Department for Education and Skills) and are reproduced under the terms of the Click-Use Licence.

First published 2008 by Folens Limited.

ISBN 978-1-85008-293-4

# Contents

Introduction                        4
Planning chart                      6
Assessment ideas                    8
Observation hints                   9

**Chapter 1: Me, myself, I**
My feelings                         10
My favourite things                 11
My ten little fingers               12
Ten fingers ✎                       13
My clean hands                      14
My style                            15
My space                            16
Dancing partners ✎                  17

**Chapter 2: Family matters**
My family                           18
Happy families ✎                    19
Family fun                          20
Family snaps                        21
Family features                     22
Shape face ✎                        23
Family feast                        24
Family figures                      25

**Chapter 3: Friends indeed**
What lovely friends                 26
Five funny friends                  27
Naming friends                      28
Anna Ant ✎                          29
A friendly face                     30
Friends in disguise ✎               31
Friend and partner                  32
Friendship stop                     33

**Chapter 4: Let's celebrate**
It's my party!                      34
Birthdays past and present          35
Birthday book                       36
Party invitation ✎                  37
Favourite festivals                 38
Patterned streamers ✎               39
Party games                         40
Celebration cake                    41

**Chapter 5: Everyone is special**
Special to me                       42
Special thanks                      43
Your own special way                44
Achievement badges ✎                45
Special people in special places    46
A special gift                      47
I am special                        48

# Introduction

## Who the book is for

This book forms part of the *Play Foundations* series which provides guidance for practitioners to set up quality play scenarios or activities with young children. It is written for all those working with three-, four- and five-year-old children in a variety of settings. Although many of the activities are written with nursery or school settings in mind, they can easily be adapted for childminders working with children in their homes. The book will be of particular interest to all those working within the Early Years Foundation Stage framework (EYFS). It will also be useful for parents*.

## Learning through play

The activities in this book are based on the EYFS principles:
- Each child is unique and is a competent learner from birth.
- Positive relationships ensure that children learn to be strong and independent.
- Enabling environments play a key role in extending learning and development.
- Learning and development takes many different forms and all areas are connected.

The focus of the activities is on child-initiated learning and the emphasis is on process rather than product. There are suggestions for using your guidance, your language and your support to promote the children's learning as they explore and play. Many of the activities can be enjoyed outside. Being outside has a positive impact on children's sense of well-being and can help all aspects of development.

## How to use this book

The book is divided into five chapters, each focusing on a different aspect of 'My friends and me', with each chapter demonstrating how theme-based activities can support all areas of children's learning and development.

The chapters are:
- Me, myself, I
- Family matters
- Friends indeed
- Let's celebrate
- Everyone is special.

## The activities

Each chapter has six activities, each focusing on either one or two Areas of learning and development. The activities give a specific Early learning goal for each learning focus. Most of the activities are designed for small groups of around four children, but in cases where individuals require more support, it may be relevant to work with just one or two children.

Each activity is divided into the following sections:
- To help to plan *Enabling environments*, there is a section on *Setting up*, outlining the resources needed and how to set up.
- *Getting started* describes how to organise the actual activity.
- *Let's talk!* provides ideas for talking with the children about their experiences, including questions that could be asked and how to differentiate language to suit the children's varying abilities. There are also suggestions for making the most of assessment opportunities.

- Recognising *A unique child* and *Positive relationships* means making sure that self-esteem, confidence and relationships remain positive and there are *Top tips* for doing so.
- The *Differentiation* section includes ideas for personalising the learning by adjusting each activity to make it easier for children needing more support or more challenging for others. This section will also be useful for planning inclusive activities for those children who have special or additional needs.
- *Further ideas* for each activity suggest ways of extending and enhancing learning and development opportunities.
- Photocopiable activity sheets are provided in the book and they can also be printed from the CD-ROM. They are intended to enhance children's play or to create game scenarios.
- Every activity page includes a Claude Cat box, which lists relevant resources on the CD-ROM.

## The importance of ICT

Nowadays, young children are becoming increasingly familiar with using ICT as part of their everyday experiences. Stories, rhymes and songs can be enjoyed through television and computer programs, and many early years settings have interactive whiteboard facilities. Children are surrounded by texts that combine images, sounds and words both on screen and paper and they need to learn to read images as well as print. The CD-ROM that accompanies this book provides opportunities for children to explore and become familiar with visual text, photographic and drawn still images, moving images, sound and colour.

## Using the CD-ROM

The CD-ROM has been designed for children to use with adult support.

### Claude Cat

Claude Cat gives instructions or asks questions which are designed to encourage children to verbalise their observations, ideas and understanding. This will help you to assess whether they need further support or challenge.

### The main menu

This screen has the option to select a theme.

### The theme menu

When the theme screen is displayed, you have the option of selecting different resources, for example, an interactive picture, story, rhyme or song, by clicking on the appropriate icon:

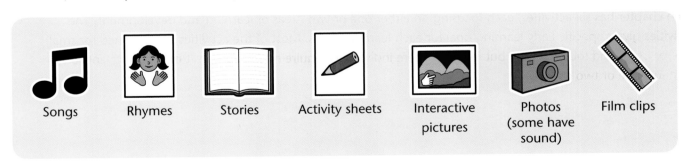

| Songs | Rhymes | Stories | Activity sheets | Interactive pictures | Photos (some have sound) | Film clips |

\* Whenever the term 'parent' is used this is taken to include parents and/or the children's primary carers.

# Planning chart

Use this chart to help with your planning. Each activity focuses on either one or two Area(s) of learning and development. These are highlighted by the stars shown on the chart. The Areas of learning and development are divided up into 'aspects' and the aspect(s) for each activity are also provided on the chart. On the activity pages you will also find an 'Early learning goal' objective for each activity.

The following key is used on the activity pages:

 PSED: Personal, social and emotional development

 CLL: Communication, language and literacy

 PSRN: Problem solving, reasoning and numeracy

 KUW: Knowledge and understanding of the world

 PD: Physical development

 CD: Creative development

| Activities | Areas of learning and development | | | | | | | |
|---|---|---|---|---|---|---|---|---|
| **Me, myself, I** | Page | PSED | CLL | PSRN | KUW | PD | CD | Aspect of learning |
| My feelings | 10 | ★ | | | | | | Dispositions and attitudes |
| My favourite things | 11 | | ★ | | | | | Language for communication |
| | | | | ★ | | | | Calculating |
| My ten little fingers | 12 | | | ★ | | | | Numbers as labels and for counting |
| | | ★ | | | | | | Making relationships |
| My clean hands | 14 | | | | ★ | | | Exploration and investigation |
| | | | ★ | | | | | Language for communication |
| My style | 15 | | | | | | ★ | Being creative – responding to experiences, expressing and communicating ideas |
| My space | 16 | | | | | ★ | | Movement and space |
| **Family matters** | Page | PSED | CLL | PSRN | KUW | PD | CD | Aspect of learning |
| My family | 18 | ★ | | | | | | Self-confidence and self-esteem |
| | | | | | | | ★ | Exploring media and materials |
| Family fun | 20 | | ★ | | | | | Language for thinking |
| | | | | ★ | | | | Numbers as labels and for counting |
| Family snaps | 21 | | | | ★ | | | Designing and making |
| | | | | | | ★ | | Using equipment and materials |
| Family features | 22 | | | ★ | | | | Calculating |
| Family feast | 24 | | | | | ★ | | Health and bodily awareness |
| Family figures | 25 | | | | | | ★ | Exploring media and materials |

My Friends and Me

| Friends indeed | Page | PSED | CLL | PSRN | KUW | PD | CD | Aspect of Learning |
|---|---|---|---|---|---|---|---|---|
| What lovely friends | 26 | ★ | | | | | | Making relationships |
| Five funny friends | 27 | | | ★ | | | | Numbers as labels and for counting |
| | | | ★ | | | | | Language for thinking |
| Naming friends | 28 | | ★ | | | | | Linking sounds and letters |
| A friendly face | 30 | | | | ★ | | | ICT |
| Friend and partner | 32 | | | | | ★ | | Using equipment and materials |
| Friendship stop | 33 | | | | | | ★ | Creating music and dance |
| | | | | | | ★ | | Movement and space |

| Let's celebrate | Page | PSED | CLL | PSRN | KUW | PD | CD | Aspect of Learning |
|---|---|---|---|---|---|---|---|---|
| It's my party! | 34 | ★ | | | | | | Behaviour and self control |
| Birthdays past and present | 35 | | | | ★ | | | Time |
| Birthday book | 36 | | ★ | | | | | Writing |
| | | ★ | | | | | | Making relationships |
| Favourite festivals | 38 | | | ★ | | | | Shape, space and measures |
| | | | ★ | | | | | Language for thinking |
| Party games | 39 | | | | | ★ | | Movement and space |
| | | | | | | | ★ | Creating music and dance |
| Celebration cake | 40 | | | | | | ★ | Developing imagination and imaginative play |

| Everyone is special | Page | PSED | CLL | PSRN | KUW | PD | CD | Aspect of Learning |
|---|---|---|---|---|---|---|---|---|
| Special to me | 42 | ★ | | | | | | Sense of community |
| | | | ★ | | | | | Language for communication |
| Special thanks | 43 | | ★ | | | | | Writing |
| Your own special way | 44 | | ★ | | | | | Language for communication |
| | | ★ | | | | | | Dispositions and attitudes |
| Special people in special places | 46 | | | | ★ | | | Place |
| A special gift | 47 | | | | | ★ | | Using equipment and materials |
| I am special | 48 | | | | | | ★ | Exploring media and materials |

# Assessment ideas

Young children are individuals first, each with a unique profile of abilities. All the planning that we do should flow from the observations that we make on an ongoing basis and these will help us to understand and consider their current interests, development and learning.

## How to assess children

Observing children during their daily routines allows us to note their responses in different situations and to different people. In some settings, a specific Area of learning and development is targeted and the key person is asked to observe what stage the children in their care have reached over the next day or week, revisiting that Area from time to time. Others use sticky notes in order to capture relevant observations. These can be collated later by a key person and entered into the ongoing records for the child. Others still make use of photography, daily diaries, activity feedback sheets or tracking records to capture the children's progress at different times. There is no prescribed method and you will find methods that suit your practice and the children and families concerned.

## Planning for assessment

Through assessment you can see what stages the children have reached in their learning and development and therefore work out the best resources, opportunities and activities to plan next. Sometimes this might involve planning a specific activity to enable the child to take their learning that little bit further, or it may be necessary to plan a similar activity in order to reinforce learning before moving on. Sometimes it will simply mean providing the right opportunities and observing the children as they play and learn independently. You will find a mixture of adult-led and child-led activities in the activity chapters with suggestions for you to observe and assess the children within the *Let's talk!* sections of each page.

## Using your assessments

Once you have observed the children at play, analyse your observations and highlight the children's achievements or their need for further support. Assessments are the decisions you make using what you have observed about each child's development and learning. You are asked to involve parents as part of the ongoing observation and assessment process and it is also helpful to share your plans for the short-term (a week) and long-term (a term) planning. Your planning should always follow the same pattern – observe, analyse and reflect, then use what you have found out to plan next steps in the child's learning. In this way you can personalise the children's learning and make the most of their strengths, interests and needs.

The 'Look, listen and note' approach of the EYFS is a helpful tool when deciding what to observe and how. On the next page, this format has been applied to children learning about 'my friends and me' so that you can begin to think about how your assessment and observations of children within this theme can feed back into your planning. For each of the five chapter headings, there are ideas for what you should look out for especially.

# Observation hints

Here are some suggestions to help you focus your observations and assessments when learning about 'my friends and me'.

| Chapter heading | Look, listen and note |
|---|---|
| **Me, myself, I** | • Observe whether individuals work in a group, or prefer to play alone.<br><br>• Listen to whether children use language imaginatively as they discuss and describe their pictures, displays and games.<br><br>• Make a note of children's movement skills as they dance or paint to music. Do they move confidently and with imagination? |
| **Family matters** | • Observe children's motivation. Do they absorb themselves in games and role-play or lose interest quickly?<br><br>• Listen to the mathematical language children use, for example, when playing with shapes in the sand, making frames and singing counting rhymes. Is it appropriate?<br><br>• Note children's responses to questions about shapes and patterns. Are they able to name and describe shapes or explain a simple pattern? |
| **Friends indeed** | • Observe how children show their feelings, for example, during music, dressing up and role-play.<br><br>• Listen and write down some of children's verbal responses to questions about the games and activities they are involved in.<br><br>• Make a note of children's physical skills as they play team games or manipulate tools in the water tray. |
| **Let's celebrate** | • Observe children's reactions as they join in with the songs and rhymes. Do they follow the actions of others or are they autonomous?<br><br>• Are the children able to recall and talk about parties, celebrations or festivals they have attended with friends and family?<br><br>• Make a note of children's comments about writing for a purpose, for example, party invitations, display labels and thank-you letters. |
| **Everyone is special** | • Observe children making cards and badges. Do they make good use of resources to express their ideas?<br><br>• Listen to children as they discuss the images on the CD-ROM. Do they make comparisons with their own cultural experiences?<br><br>• Note the descriptive or mathematical language children use as they discuss rhymes such as 'Ten special children', for example, *one less*, *take away* and *how many?* |

# Me, myself, I — My feelings

## Setting up

Watch the film clip of an artist at work together and talk about the scene with the children, encouraging them to describe their observations. Secure large sheets of plain paper, card or fabric to the ground outside and place several pots of paint there. Provide the children with aprons and a variety of painting tools, for example, wide and narrow paint brushes, sponges, damp cloths and palettes. Place a tape/CD player in a safe place, near by.

## Getting started

- Play a tape/CD either of the children's favourite tunes and songs or some new songs or unfamiliar tunes. If possible, select tunes with a range of instrumental changes, for example, fast beats, slow beats, repeated rhythms, crescendos (getting louder) and diminuendos (getting softer).
- Invite the children to express their thoughts, feelings or emotions by painting free-style to the music as it plays.
- Ask, *Does this song/tune make you feel happy, excited, sad or calm? What colours make you feel happy, sad, excited or calm? Do you enjoy fast tunes or slow tunes best? Would you paint fast to match a fast tune? How would you paint to loud music?*
- Display the paintings on the wall and invite the children to each think of original titles for their work.

## Let's talk!

Ask, *What colours does the artist use in the film clip? Can you describe some of the shapes and patterns created by the artist?* For children requiring more support, ask *Do you like painting? What type of pictures do you have on the wall at home? What is your favourite colour?* For children requiring challenge ask, *What tools is the artist using to create the painting?* Are the children interested in the film clip? Are they keen to talk about their own views and experiences? Are the children eager to join in new activities? Are they generally motivated and willing to learn?

## Top tip

Help boost the children's self-esteem by encouraging them to sign their paintings with pride like a professional artist! Invite parents into your setting to admire the children's paintings.

## Differentiation

Encourage less confident children to have a go by offering them a small sheet of paper, card or fabric for their first attempt at expressive painting. Challenge those who require further stimulation by inviting them to mix their own colours in advance.

## Further ideas

- Invite the children to use finger painting to create expressive pictures on a smaller scale.
- Encourage the children to join in expressive, free-style dance to the same songs and tunes.

# My favourite things

## CD-ROM resources

 Teddy bear collection

 Five favourite toys

**Early learning goals**

Enjoy listening to and using spoken and written language, and readily turn to it in their play and learning.

Begin to relate addition to combining two groups of objects and subtraction to 'taking away'.

## Setting up

Look at the photo of the boy and his teddy bear collection on the CD-ROM and talk about it with the children. Invite them to bring examples or pictures of their favourite things into your setting.

## Getting started

- Invite the children to help organise a simple exhibition in your setting showing examples or pictures of the children's favourite objects or collections, such as a stamp collector's album or a small selection of teddies or shells from the beach. Observe and talk about interesting features within each collection and encourage the owner of each collection to express and explain their enthusiasm for the objects they have bought in.
- Listen to the rhyme 'Five favourite toys' on the CD-ROM together. Provide each child with five small world toys in a bag and encourage them to join in with the words, removing one of the toys from their bags with each verse. Finally, ask the children to make all five toys reappear! Invite the children to use the rhyme to inspire imaginative play in the home corner.

## Let's talk!

Ask, *What has the boy in the photo collected? What collections are in our exhibition? What would you like to collect?* For children requiring more support ask, *Which is your favourite collection in the exhibition?* For children requiring challenge ask, *Are all the items in the photo the same size, colour and shape?* Notice how the children use the exhibition and rhyme to inspire discussion and imaginative play.

## Top tip

Encourage the children to respect one another's collections by emphasising that every collection is unique and special to the collector. Support developing relationships by encouraging the children to show an interest in each other's collections by asking questions and by making positive comments.

## Differentiation

Listen to the rhyme several times with those who require more support so they become familiar with the words and the count down from five to zero. Challenge those who require further stimulation by inviting them to label their collection with words and information, for example, the name of the collector, how many items are in the collection and what inspired the collection.

## Further ideas

- Encourage the children to join in role-play based on packing up favourite things to go on holiday. *What would you need for a camping trip? For a stay at granny's house?*

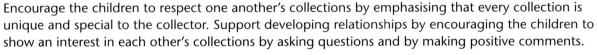

# My ten little fingers

## CD-ROM resources

 Ten fingers

### Early learning goals

Recognise numerals 1 to 9.

Work as part of a group or class, taking turns and sharing fairly, understanding that there needs to be agreed values and codes of behaviour for groups of people, including adults and children, to work together harmoniously.

## Setting up

Photocopy the activity sheet 'Ten fingers' on page 13 or print it from the CD-ROM for each child.

## Getting started

- Encourage the children to look at the pictures and numbers on the activity sheet to help them sing the following rhyme to the tune of 'Ten in a bed'. Invite the children to wriggle the appropriate number of fingers as they sing:

  *I have ten little fingers, and they all do this, wriggle, wriggle; wriggle, wriggle!*
  *Now it's time for one to go, I have nine little fingers, and they all do this, wriggle, wriggle; wriggle, wriggle!*

- Continue in this way for eight, seven, six, five, four, three and two fingers and then sing the final verse:

  *I have one little finger, and it's on its own, wriggle, wriggle; wriggle, wriggle!*
  *Now it's time for one to go, I have no little fingers, then ten do this, wriggle, wriggle; wriggle, wriggle!*

- Complete the song by inviting the children to hold both hands up high while wriggling all ten fingers.

## Let's talk!

Point to the numerals on the activity sheet and ask questions such as, *What number is this? Can you show me this number of fingers?* For children requiring more support, ask *Where is the number three on your activity sheet?* For children requiring challenge, ask *What number comes before four? What number comes after six?* Note when the children are able to recognise numerals 1 to 9 with confidence.

## Top tip

Prompt less confident children by helping them to count the appropriate number of fingers to wriggle between each verse. Support developing relationships by encouraging the children to help one another count, match and compare wriggling fingers!

## Differentiation

Cut the activity sheet in half to show five fingers labelled 1 to 5 for those who require more support and adapt the song accordingly. Challenge those who require further stimulation by inviting them to predict what number will come next in the song.

## Further ideas

- Help the children to thread one to ten small items or pictures on to ten lengths of thick wool labelled with bold numerals to create a counting mobile for your setting.
- Sing traditional counting rhymes with the children, such as 'Five little speckled frogs', 'Ten green bottles' and 'Ten fat sausages'.

# Ten fingers

Look at the numbers as you sing the song 'I have ten little fingers'

1 2 3 4 5 6 7 8 9 10

Wriggle wriggle wriggle wriggle wriggle

# My clean hands

### CD-ROM resources

Soapy hands

### Early learning goals

Look closely at similarities, differences, patterns and change.

Extend their vocabulary, exploring the meanings and sounds of new words.

### Setting up

Look at the photo of soapy hands on the CD-ROM and talk about washing our hands. Set up a bowl of water, hand-washing equipment and aprons outdoors, along with plastic jugs, cups, pots, spoons and other implements for pouring, stirring and whisking near by. Provide child-friendly bubble bath (be aware of children with sensitive skin or conditions).

### Getting started

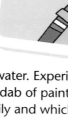

- Invite the children to pour, stir, whisk and ripple the water with their hands and using the jugs and implements. Talk about the feel, sound and appearance of the water, encouraging descriptive language such as *trickle, shimmer, splash, clear, dribble* and *drip*.
- After outdoor or messy play invite them to have a go at washing their dirty hands in bowls of plain water. Experiment with different types of harmless dirt, for example, a dab of paint, a sprinkling of flour or a melted chocolate button. Which type of dirt washes off easily and which types of dirt are hard to remove?
- Invite the children to add the bubble bath liquid to the water. Encourage them to notice differences and changes as they pour, stir, whisk and ripple the water. Invite them to wash their dirty hands this time in bowls of soapy water. Does the dirt wash off more easily with soap? Invite the children to experiment and explore using different types of dirt as before. Talk with the children about their observations and encourage descriptive words such as *bubbly, sparkling, slippery, shiny, glisten, clean* and *soapy*.

### Let's talk!

Ask, *How can you tell if the water is clean or dirty?* For children requiring more support, ask *What happens to the water if you wash dirty hands in it?* For children requiring challenge, ask *What changes happen when bubbles are added to the water?* Notice the children who are gaining an awareness of observing and describing similarities, differences, patterns and change.

### Top tip

Encourage the children to whisk, pour and splash the water with due care and attention for others near by. Develop positive relationships by asking the children to share equipment and to help one another experiment and explore.

### Differentiation

Help those who require more support by providing one-to-one assistance during the hand-washing stages. Challenge those who require further stimulation by inviting them to help clean up effectively and cooperatively, using a range of mops, sponges, buckets and towels.

### Further ideas

- Use a marbling kit to create bubble print pictures.
- Help the children to blow bubbles through their fingers or use a commercial pot of bubbles with a blowing loop.

# My style

**Early learning goal**

Respond in a variety of ways to what they see, hear, smell, touch and feel.

## Setting up

View the film clip of the windwheel on the CD-ROM and talk about the colours and how they blend together. Outdoors, provide pots of paint (red, blue and yellow), sheets of paper, brushes, colour-mixing palettes and pots of water, PVA glue or cornflour to thicken the paint, old perfume, crushed garlic or almond essence (smell), tiny beads, wood shavings and sand (texture). Be aware of any allergies to materials.

## Getting started

- Invite the children to experiment by mixing paints to discover a colour that they like, that matches how they feel or to reflect their personality. Alternatively, help them to explore making purple, orange and green by mixing the colours together in pairs. Encourage them to find out what happens if they mix all three primary colours together. What happens if they mix the new colours together? Encourage them to paint a picture, a pattern or random marks using their new colours.
- Invite the children to extend their explorations by creating colours with different textures, consistencies and smells using the products on offer. Invite the children to use the mixtures to create patterns or pictures and display them on the wall with suitable titles: 'Feely, smelly patterns', 'I did it my way' or 'My style'.

## Let's talk!

Ask, *How does it feel to create a brand new colour?* For children requiring more support, ask *Have you made orange, purple or green?* For children requiring challenge, ask, *How did you make brown? How would you change green to brown?* Notice how the children respond to what they see, hear, smell, touch and feel. Are they able to describe their experiences? Are they willing to explore and experiment by using a range of tools and materials?

## Top tip

Ensure that every child feels proud of their new colours by inviting the peer group to make positive comments or by working as a team to think of interesting names for the colours. Invite parents into your setting to view an exhibition of the paintings.

## Differentiation

Help those who require more support by making suggestions or by helping with practical challenges such as selecting suitable tools, adding ingredients or stirring the mixtures. Challenge those who require further stimulation by inviting them to 'write' the ingredients for one of their new mixtures.

## Further ideas

- Encourage several children to work together to create a patchwork pattern using shades of paint they have created themselves.
- Set up a 'Make and mix' resource area to store materials for creative and messy play, for example, beads, buttons, threads, wool, pebbles, wood shavings, sand, sawdust, feathers, seeds and sequins.

# My space

**CD-ROM resources**

Dancing partners

Children dancing

**Early learning goal**

Move with confidence, imagination and in safety.

## Setting up

Organise a place outside where the children can move freely and safely to music. Observe and talk about the photo of the two girls dressed as fairies dancing on the CD-ROM.

## Getting started

- Invite the children to dance free-style by listening to the rhythm and beat of different types of music, for example, jazz, pop and classical. Include tunes that are likely to be familiar to the children as well as less familiar tunes.
- Encourage them to respond to the music with different facial expressions, for example, happy faces for cheery music, looking sad for solemn music and excited for energetic music.
- Suggest that they create different body movements according to the sound of the music, for example, skipping, hopping, jumping and twirling.
- Provide the children with props to help them make up interesting dance routines, for example, ribbons or streamers to flap, wave and twirl, or colourful and frilly 'pompoms' to swirl, shimmer and shake.

## Let's talk!

Ask, *What is your favourite style of dance? What is the difference between ballet and tap dancing?* For children requiring more support, ask *Why do you like dancing?* For children requiring challenge, ask *How does dancing make you feel?* Be aware of children who move with increasing confidence, with imagination and in safety.

## Top tip

Ensure that every child joins in, for example, supporting shy children or children with special physical needs by becoming their dancing partner. Develop positive relationships by encouraging the children to dance cooperatively in pairs or small groups.

## Differentiation

Dance alongside those who require more support. Challenge those who require further stimulation by inviting them to perform a short dance or sequence of movements to the rest of the group.

## Further ideas

- Print a copy of the 'Girls dancing' photo on the CD-ROM to display in a convenient location. Use the image to inspire discussion about the children's dancing experiences, for example, favourite forms of dance, hobby or past-time dances or dances that have close links to family traditions, customs or festivals.
- Provide the children with a copy of the activity sheet 'Dancing partners' from page 17 or printed from the CD-ROM. Help them to cut out the pictures and to match the dancers by the pattern on their outfits. Alternatively, print several card copies of the activity sheet from the CD-ROM to create playing cards for games such as 'snap' and 'pairs'.

# Dancing partners

Cut out the pictures and match the dancers by their patterns.

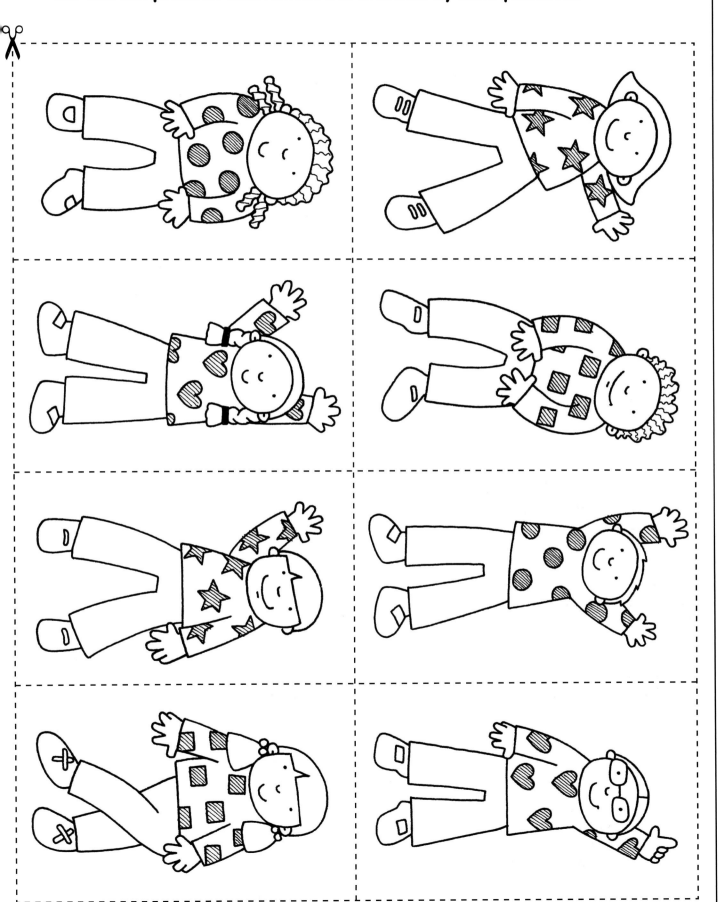

# Family matters  My family

**CD-ROM resources**

Happy families

**Early learning goals**

Respond to significant experiences, showing a range of feelings when appropriate.

Explore colour, texture, shape, form and space in two or three dimensions.

### Setting up

Talk with the children about their family (be sensitive to all family groupings). Provide each child with a large sheet of card, several small sheets of paper, pens, pencils and glue. Invite children to bring in photos of individual members of their family, or people they live with (optional).

### Getting started

- Ask the children to draw a portrait of themselves (or use a photo) to glue in the centre of a large sheet of card. Invite the children to draw pictures or collect photos of other people in their family to glue around the picture of themself. Some children may wish to include pictures of family pets. Help the children to label each picture with the name of the person or pet. When complete, invite each child to talk about the people or pets on their 'Happy families' picture boards.
- Encourage the children to help organise and host a family viewing session of their work.

### Let's talk!

Ask, *How many people are in your family? What sort of things do you and your family enjoy doing together?* For children requiring more support, ask *Whose picture is on your 'Happy families' picture board? Do you have any pets?* For children requiring challenge, ask *What makes a happy family?* Notice the children's responses during the activity, for example, do they join in discussions with interest and enthusiasm? Are they willing to recall significant family events? Do they listen to the experiences of others?

### Top tip

Encourage every child to express why they are proud of their family, proud of individuals within the family or proud of themselves, for example, *I am proud of my sister because she helps my mum.* Support developing relationships by emphasising the importance of listening attentively to one another and by taking turns to speak.

### Differentiation

Emphasise, to those who require more support, that the drawings they produce for the 'Happy families' picture board are for fun, they do not need to look exactly like the real people or pets! Challenge those who require further stimulation by inviting them to use a mirror to create a self-portrait.

### Further ideas

- Copy the activity sheet 'Happy families' on page 19 or print it from the CD-ROM on to card. Invite the children to colour in and cut out the 16 pictures to create a set of cards to play a simple version of 'Happy families'.
- Invite families into your setting to talk to the children about family life in the past, bringing photos to show them.

# Happy families

Cut out all 16 cards to play card games.

# Family fun

## CD-ROM resources

Pitching a tent

Ten cousins camping

## Early learning goals

Use language to imagine and recreate roles and experiences.

Say and use number names in order in familiar contexts.

## Setting up

View the film clip 'Pitching a tent' on the CD-ROM and talk about the scene with the children. If possible pitch a small tent in the grounds of your setting or make a fabric den in the role-play area. Invite the children to use the tent or den for imaginative play about being on a camping holiday.

## Getting started

- Talk about the different types of holiday that people go on and the different accommodation they stay in, for example, a hotel, a caravan or a tent.
- Listen to the rhyme 'Ten cousins camping' on the CD-ROM.
- Encourage the children to mime the actions of campers, for example, hammering in the tent pegs, unrolling a sleeping bag or pumping up the air-beds as everyone sings the words to the rhyme to the tune of 'Ten green bottles'. Ask one child to pretend to be the cousin who went home. Then continue the mime and song until there are no campers left!

## Let's talk!

Talk to the children about their pretend camping holiday in the role-play tent or den. Ask questions such as, *What did you enjoy about your holiday?* For children requiring support, ask *How did you get there?* For children requiring a challenge, ask *Can you describe a favourite holiday or a special day out with friends or family.* Notice the children's ability and confidence in explaining their holiday memories or role-play experiences.

## Top tip

Ensure that every child has a turn playing in the tent or den, for example, encourage shy or less confident children to choose an older child or best friend as a 'play buddy'. Develop positive relationships by inviting small groups of children to make up role-play scenes to perform in front of their peers, staff or parents. Encourage the actors to bow at the end of their performance and the audience to clap to show their appreciation.

## Differentiation

Join in with the role-play scenes or prompt ideas for those who require more support. Challenge those who require further stimulation by inviting them to adapt the words to the rhyme 'Ten cousins camping' for example, 'Ten friends fishing', 'Ten brothers boating' or 'Ten sisters snorkelling'.

## Further ideas

- Encourage the children to imagine what it would be like to sleep in a tent over night. Ask questions such as, *What type of equipment would you need? What outdoor sounds might you hear?*
- Listen to the words of the rhyme on the CD-ROM several times to help the children learn them.

# Family snaps

 **CD-ROM resources**

At the seaside

 **Early learning goals**

Select the tools and techniques they need to shape, assemble and join materials they are using.

Handle tools, objects, construction and malleable materials safely and with increasing control.

## Setting up

Observe the photo of the parent and child at the seaside on the CD-ROM and talk about the scene with the children. Invite them to bring in recent or historical family photos to display on the wall. Gather together: coloured card, paper, child scissors, straws, adhesive tape, feathers, paper doilies, child-safe hole-punch, PVA glue, foil, shiny paper, crêpe paper, coloured sand, tissue paper, sequins, ribbons, lace, dried pasta, small shells, scraps of fabric, glitter and so on.

## Getting started

- Help the children to scan or photocopy the family photos and invite them to make a personalised or themed frame for their photo by cutting a cardboard shape around them and decorating the edges using craft materials.
- Encourage the children to create an individual design, for example: a photo of a family on the beach could be decorated with tiny shells, coloured sand and blue glitter to represent the sea; a photo of a family walk could be decorated with paper flowers, feathers and gold paper to represent the sun.
- Display the photos in the frames or invite the children to take them home as a gift for someone special.

## Let's talk!

Ask, *What does your photo show? What shape would you like your frame to be?* For children requiring more support, ask *What colours and materials would you like to use on your frame?* For children requiring challenge, ask *Can you describe how you would like your frame to look?* Note those who select tools and techniques with confidence.

## Top tip

Encourage the children to value one another's choice of photo or decorative frame by emphasising that some photos are very personal and the memories or feelings they inspire might not seem obvious to others. Encourage developing relationships by inviting older children to help younger children use the tools and decorative materials with confidence and flair.

## Differentiation

Provide practical help such as cutting cardboard, trimming adhesive tape and spreading glue for those who require more support. Challenge those who require further stimulation by inviting them to draw a plan of their frame or to make a list of the materials they might need.

## Further ideas

- Invite the children to decorate a personalised shape to make a wall plaque for someone in their family such as a fish shape for a grandad who enjoys fishing.

# Family features

**CD-ROM resources**

Shape face

**Early learning goal**

In practical activities and discussion, begin to use the vocabulary involved in adding and subtracting.

## Setting up

Photocopy the activity sheet 'Shape face' from page 23 or print it from the CD-ROM for each child. Place a wide variety of colourful plastic or cardboard shapes in the sand tray outdoors.

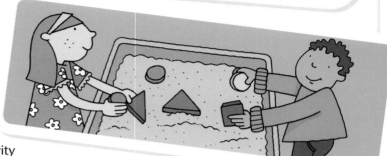

## Getting started

- Provide each child with a copy of the activity sheet and encourage them to name and identify the six shapes used in the picture. Help them to count the shapes on the face (using the number line if necessary) and to write the totals in the appropriate spaces. Invite the children to colour in the shapes on the sheet.
- Suggest that the children use the shapes in the sand tray to create an imaginary face representing someone in their family. Emphasise that the face is for fun and does not have to look like the person, in fact the funnier the better!
- Help the children to count and compare how many shapes they used to create the image, for example, two blue circles for eyes, six brown triangles for hair, one pink oval for the nose.
- Invite the children to add or remove shapes to create a different image.

## Let's talk!

Look at the activity sheet with the children and ask, *How many hearts are there on the face? Can you see more than five triangles?* Count the shapes with children requiring more support. For children requiring challenge, ask *If two hearts were rubbed out, how many hearts would be left?* Note those children who are beginning to use vocabulary such as, *add, take away, one more, subtract,* and *equal.*

## Top tip

Encourage the children to collaborate with one another, respecting all the images and designs. Reinforce developing relationships by encouraging the children to make positive comments about one another's sand pictures, for example, *I like the way you have used a triangle shape for the nose. What a good idea to use matching shapes for the eyes.*

## Differentiation

Point and count the shapes with those who require more support. Challenge those who require further stimulation by inviting them to add extra shapes to the face before they fill in the grid at the bottom of the activity sheet.

## Further ideas

- Suggest that the children colour all matching shapes on the activity sheet using the same colour, for example, all the hearts pink, the circles blue and the squares yellow.
- Offer 'Face shape' challenges by suggesting the children make a face in the sand using a specific number of shapes, for example: one circle, two squares, three triangles and four hexagons.

**Count the shapes on the face and write the numbers in the box.**

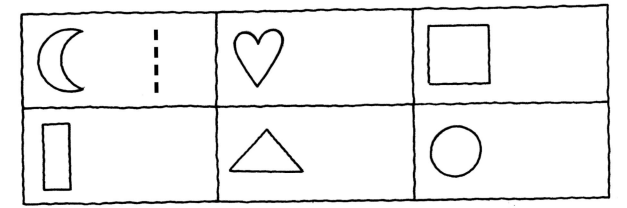

# Family feast

**Early learning goal**
Recognise the importance of keeping healthy, and those things which contribute to this.

*LEARNING AND DEVELOPMENT*

*ENABLING ENVIRONMENTS*

## Setting up

Observe and talk about the photo of an allotment on the CD-ROM. Prepare an area outside for planting or place compost in large patio containers.

## Getting started

- Listen to the story 'The Wellbeings' vegetable patch' on the CD-ROM with the children and talk about what happened in the story. Encourage the children to recall, from the story, what plants need to help them grow, for example, water and sunlight.
- Help the children to plant some easy-to-grow salad vegetables such as tomatoes, lettuce, radishes, carrots and beetroot in a prepared area of soil or in large patio containers in the grounds of your setting. Encourage them to water, weed and care for the plants on a regular basis and invite them to take it in turns to pick some of the vegetables when they have fully grown.
- Invite parents, grandparents or relatives into your setting for a 'family feast' of salad vegetables grown and prepared by the children. Alternatively, invite the parents into your setting to help the children pick, wash, trim and dress the salad for a group picnic outdoors. (Check allergies and seek parental permission before the children eat anything.)
- Use the activity to help develop the children's awareness about healthy eating, including the recommended five fruit and vegetables a day.

## Let's talk!

Ask, *What have you planted? How did you plant your vegetables? How are you going to care for your plants?* For children requiring more support, ask *What are your favourite fruit and vegetables?* For children requiring challenge, ask *Which is more healthy, an apple or a sugary sweet? Why are fruit and vegetables good for us?* During discussions notice those children who are beginning to recognise the importance of keeping healthy, and those things which contribute to this.

*A UNIQUE CHILD*

*POSITIVE RELATIONSHIPS*

## Top tip

Help each child write a special name label to stick in the soil to help them recall what they planted and where. Provide adapted tools for children with special physical needs. Invite parents or grandparents who are keen gardeners to talk to the children.

## Differentiation

Help those who require more support by providing one-to-one assistance as they plant, weed, water and harvest their produce. Challenge those who require further stimulation by inviting them to record the height and width of each plant as it grows.

## Further ideas

- Arrange a visit to an allotment or vegetable patch during different stages of growth.
- Invite the children to photograph their vegetables during the planting, growing and harvesting stages. Display the pictures in a book with captions and comments from the children.

# Family figures

**Early learning goal**

Explore colour, texture, shape, form and space in two or three dimensions.

## Setting up

Listen to the rhyme 'Helping hands' on the CD-ROM and encourage the children to think about the help, kindness and love shown to them by their friends and family. Set up a clay modelling area outdoors.

## Getting started

- Invite the children to use the clay to create a model representing a kind, thoughtful or helpful person they know. Emphasise that the model does not need to look like a real person.
- Encourage the children to explore the texture of the clay as they work by rolling, squelching, patting, rubbing, smoothing, cutting and modelling it into shape.
- When the clay is thoroughly dry, invite the children to paint their model. Leave the paint to dry, and then help them to coat the model in PVA glue to create a shiny surface. Display the models in your setting before the children take them home.

## Let's talk!

Ask, *What are you making with the clay? What does the clay feel like?* For children requiring support, ask *Why do you enjoy squashing, rolling, patting and squeezing the clay?* For children requiring challenge, ask *What or who does your shape look like?* Notice the children who are keen to explore shape, form and texture and note those who are keen to describe their model, perhaps using their hands to help highlight 3D shapes that are difficult to describe.

## Top tip

Provide plenty of time for each child to explore, experiment and play freely with the clay, before they attempt to make models, to help boost their confidence and ability to manipulate the material successfully. Invite parents into your setting to admire the models on display.

## Differentiation

Provide those who require more support with a small lump of clay. Challenge those who require further stimulation by inviting them to construct simple texture-making tools using stiff card to create feely patterns on their model, for example, zigzag shapes cut into the edge of card can be used to scrape ridges and criss-cross patterns in the clay, and rolled and folded card can be pressed into the clay to make circular patterns and folded card can be pressed into the clay to make patterns.

## Further ideas

- Suggest that the children make up additional verses to the rhyme by substituting the word 'dad' for the name of a friend or family member.
- Encourage the children to make up mimes as they sing, such as sweeping arms back and forth in the air to represent cleaning windows.

# Friends indeed

## What lovely friends

**Early learning goal**

Work as part of a group or class, taking turns and sharing fairly, understanding that there needs to be agreed values and codes of behaviour for groups of people, including adults and children, to work together harmoniously.

### Setting up

Set up a 'Listening and sound-making area' in your setting with a CD player and a range of percussion instruments, such as drum, tambourine, bells and shakers. Listen to the rhyme 'Twinkle, twinkle I can see' on the CD-ROM.

### Getting started

- Invite the children to share the percussion instruments as they sing the song 'Twinkle, twinkle I can see' to the tune of 'Twinkle, twinkle little star'.
- Invite the children to recall and talk about acts of kindness shown to them by their friends. Encourage the children to explain why being kind is important and help them to consider how they can be kind to their peers in your setting, for example, helping new children to settle in, playing with lonely children, sharing toys and playing games fairly.
- Encourage the children to draw or paint a picture of a kind friend or group of friends. Help the children to write a short sentence about the person in their picture. Display the pictures and captions on the wall under a heading such as 'Friendship gallery', 'Kind friends' or 'What lovely friends'.

### Let's talk!

Ask questions such as, *Does your favourite game involve taking turns? Are you good at taking turns?* For children requiring more support, ask *Who do you share your toys with at home?* For children requiring challenge, ask *Why is it important to take turns? Is it important to play by the rules?* Help those children who need extra support and encouragement to share or play fairly. Acknowledge children who work well as part of a group and play cooperatively with their peers.

### Top tip

Ensure that every child is included in the 'Friendship gallery' by prompting the children to recall recent acts of kindness shown by each member of the group. Invite the parents to visit the 'Friendship gallery' with their children.

### Differentiation

Sing along with those who require more support. Challenge those who require further stimulation by inviting them to make up new words to the song 'Twinkle, twinkle I can see'.

### Further ideas

- Look at the photo of the two children with a book on the CD-ROM. Talk about the picture and encourage the children to describe their favourite games and pastimes.
- Invite the children to be a 'special friend' to a younger child or set up a 'buddy' system so that all new children to your setting have a 'special person' to show them around.

# Five funny friends

## Setting up

Set up a role-play area indoors or outdoors with a selection of fancy dress and comical items, for example, false moustaches, zany glasses, glittery wigs, silly hats and so on. Listen to the song 'Five funny friends' on the CD-ROM with the children.

## Getting started

- Encourage a group of five children to wear items of fancy dress to represent 'Five funny friends' and to make up actions as everyone sings the first verse of the song. After the first verse encourage one of the five to walk away *to see their mum*. Continue singing the song and then encourage a second child to walk away *to see their mum*.
- Continue in this way until one child is left, then sing the words:

  *One funny friend is here with me; Waving and jumping merrily;*
  *Now he/she's gone home to see his/her mum, So there's no more*
  *friends, it's not much fun!*
- Ask the last child to walk away. Now everyone should sing:

  *No funny friends are here with me; Waving and jumping merrily;*
  *But, look who's coming back for fun, My five funny friends*
  *and every single mum!*
- Encourage all five children to return with a partner to represent their mum!

## Let's talk!

During different stages of the activity ask questions such as *How many funny friends can you see? How many funny friends have gone away?* For children requiring more support, ask *How many funny friends are wearing silly hats?* For children requiring challenge ask *How many funny friends will be left if two more walk away?* Notice those who can count to five with confidence and those who need help to say and use number names in order.

## Top tip

Ensure that every child can join in, for example, by adapting the song to suit children with specific physical needs by substituting the word *jumping* for *clapping*, *spinning*, *bouncing* and so on. Reinforce positive relationships by dressing up yourself as a 'funny friend' and joining in with the actions.

## Differentiation

Start the song with the words 'Three funny friends' for those who require more support. Challenge children by singing about 'Ten funny friends' using ten puppets as props for counting.

## Further ideas

- Encourage the children to use the fancy dress items to join in imaginative play based on the theme of 'Funny friends'.
- Help the children to make simple hand or stick puppets based on the theme of 'Funny friends', using recycled materials such as paper bags, boxes, strips of stiff card, fabric and paper cups.

# Naming friends

### Early learning goals

Link sounds to letters, naming and sounding the letters of the alphabet.

### Setting up
Set up a role-play area outdoors with dressing-up clothes and props for the children to create a range of different characters, for example, hats, coats, wigs, walking sticks, handbags, briefcases, glasses and so on.

### Getting started
- Encourage the children to work with a friend by helping one another to dress up as an imaginary character using props such as hats, cloaks, glasses and wigs.
- When dressed up, encourage each child to make up a simple name for their friend using the fancy dress props as an initial letter guide, for example, '**S**uzie Long **S**ocks', '**B**ertie **B**ig **B**oots' and '**F**iona **F**rilly Dress'.
- Invite groups of children to use the made-up names during imaginative play to bring the characters 'alive', for example, '**S**uzie Long **S**ocks' invites '**B**ertie **B**ig **B**oots' to a party.
- Encourage the children to explore a range of humorous scenarios for role-play. Alternatively, prompt ideas to help set the scene. Suggest they repeat the activity by changing their fancy dress clothing and making up new names for one another. Listen to the children as they play and help those children who need assistance in identifying initial phonemes (letter sounds) or who need guidance when choosing a name for each role-play character.

### Let's talk!
Ask, *What would you call someone wearing these baggy trousers?* For children requiring more support, ask *What does your character's name begin with?* Ask children needing further challenge, *Can you think of two or more names beginning with 'L'?* Look out for those children who need additional help in linking phonemes to letters. Introduce 'blending' to children who know the initial phonemes, for example, 't' and 'r' make 'tr' as in 'train', 'tree' and 'trip'.

### Top tip
Help the children to feel confident by involving their parents as much as possible, for example, invite the parents to an 'open session' at your setting so they can observe and appreciate the variety of interesting activities enjoyed by their children as they learn the initial phonemes and letter names.

### Differentiation
Encourage children who need additional support to say and identify the initial phoneme and letter name of their friends' names, for example, 'p' for Peter, 's' for Sita. Challenge those who require further stimulation by inviting them to write and say the letter sounds.

### Further ideas
- Use the photocopiable activity sheet 'Anna Ant' on page 29 or print it from the CD-ROM to help the children identify the correct phoneme to match each letter name.
- Ask the children to make up a name for each smiley character on the activity sheet, for example, 'Bob the banana', 'Clare the carrot' and 'Fred the fish'.

# A friendly face

**CD-ROM resources**

Friends in disguise

Changing faces

**Early learning goal**

Find out about and identify the uses of everyday technology and use information and communication technology and programmable toys to support their learning.

## Setting up
Source a simple painting program for the computer in your setting. Show the children how to use a colour printer. Display books and pictures showing portraits by different artists (such as Picasso) and photographers.

## Getting started
- Look at the portraits with the children and talk about the different styles and techniques. Invite the children to create a portrait of their friend using a painting program on the computer. Emphasise that the picture can have eyes, nose, and mouth wherever they want them to go and using any colours.
- Encourage the children to explore and experiment with the painting program by adding and changing shapes and colours as they work. When the children are happy with the image on the screen help them to print a colour copy of the portrait.
- Invite the children to display their pictures on the wall under a heading such as 'Portrait gallery' 'Friendly faces' or 'Friendly features'.

## Let's talk!
Ask, *Can you tell me who you've drawn a picture of?* Support by talking about the colours, *You've chosen green eyes*. Extend by asking, *What shapes have you used?* During the activity notice how confidently and competently the children handle the mouse and keyboard.

## Top tip
Help each child feel special by sharing a smile with them. Talk about the importance of a friendly smile and ask the children how a smile makes them feel, for example, welcome, happy, pleased. Encourage a friendly, relaxed environment by promoting the effects of a smile and lead by example.

## Differentiation
Provide one-to-one assistance for those who are less familiar with a computer mouse and keyboard. Challenge those who require further stimulation by inviting them to include detailed features on their computer screen portrait, for example, eyebrows, ears, eyelashes, hairclips, earrings and so on.

## Further ideas
- Help the children to use the interactive picture 'Changing faces' on the CD-ROM. They can drag and drop the food to make funny faces.
- Help the children to use a digital camera to complete the activity sheet 'Friends in disguise' on page 31 or print from the CD-ROM. Talk about the rhyme on the activity sheet: *This is my friend and this is me. But in our masks can you see, who is my friend and who is me?*

# Friends in disguise

Place photos of you and your friend in the top two spaces.

Place photos of you and your friend in disguise in the bottom two spaces.

## This is my friend and this is me.

But in our masks can you see,
who is my friend and who is me?

# Friend and partner

**CD-ROM resources**

Friends playing

**Early learning goal**

Use a range of small and large equipment.

## Setting up

Place a large water tray outdoors and ask the children to help collect small and large objects for placing in a water tray, for example, plastic bricks, real stones and pebbles, plastic cups and saucers, beads, plastic food, real or pretend coins, small world toys such as boats, fish and submarines. Place spoons, spades, scoops, tongs, tubs and tweezers near by.

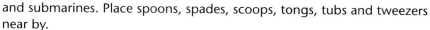

## Getting started

- Watch the film clip on the CD-ROM of the two children playing on the beach and ask: *What are they playing with? Are they playing together?*
- Ask the children to drop objects of different shapes and sizes into the water tray and invite them to use the scooping tools to retrieve the objects. Encourage them to investigate which tools are best for collecting small objects, big objects, heavy objects, flat objects and so on.
- Encourage the children to team up with a friend and invite each pair to play games based on helping their partner to collect objects out of the water without using their hands.
- Alternatively, invite each pair of children to play 'Scoop share': ask each pair of children to select one scooping tool and encourage them to retrieve one object out of the water by sharing the same tool. Encourage the children to make up their own games.

## Let's talk!

Ask, *Which objects are floating and which have sunk? Which objects are easy to scoop out of the water and which are difficult?* Ask children needing support, *Which scoop is the easiest to use?* Ask children requiring further challenge, *Why are some objects more difficult to scoop out than others?* During play, notice the children who explore and practice handling a wide range of tools and equipment. Support and encourage those who repeatedly select the same scooping tools or avoid retrieving objects that require patience or practice.

## Top tip

Ensure every child can join in, for example, provide tools with adapted handles or offer 'hand-over-hand' support for children with specific physical needs. Invite parents to attend a 'Fun and games' session so they can find out how their children learn as they play.

## Differentiation

Play alongside those who require more support or guidance. Challenge those who require further stimulation by inviting them to scoop up a certain number of objects in a given time.

## Further ideas

- Invite the children to use small and large equipment to play games such as scooping toys out of a sand pit, retrieving teddies from a basket or placing play food in a pretend cooking pot.
- During play, encourage the children to explore and experiment using all the scooping tools on offer.

# Friendship stop

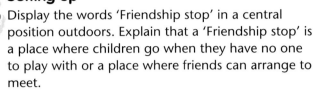

**CD-ROM resources**

The Grand Old Duke of York

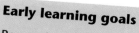
**Early learning goals**

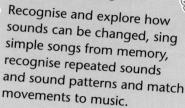

Recognise and explore how sounds can be changed, sing simple songs from memory, recognise repeated sounds and sound patterns and match movements to music.

Show awareness of space, of themselves and of others.

## Setting up

Display the words 'Friendship stop' in a central position outdoors. Explain that a 'Friendship stop' is a place where children go when they have no one to play with or a place where friends can arrange to meet.

## Getting started

- Ask up to ten children to stand in a circle or around the outer edge of the outdoor area. Elect a leader to mime the actions of a bus driver by manoeuvring, on foot, around the outdoor area.
- Ask the leader to select one child to follow them by pretending to be a passenger. Ask everyone to sing: *One friend on the (bus) follows me, follows me, follows me. One friend on the (bus) follows me, all round here.* To the tune of 'The wheels on the bus'. Ask the first passenger to swiftly select a second passenger as everyone sings the second verse: *Two friends on the (bus) follow me and so on.*
- The second passenger should select a third passenger as everyone sings the third verse. Continue in this way until all the children are following the leader.
- Sing the final verse and encourage the leader to stop in the appropriate place for all the passengers to 'get off' the imaginary bus to play, skip, dance or run freely.

## Let's talk!

Ask, *What could you call this game? Could you add sound effects to the song?* Ask children needing more support, *Have you been on a bus before?* Suggest to children requiring more challenge, *Could you make up a new verse?* Encourage the children to sing the song from memory as they pretend to drive a vehicle. Introduce the children to other games that are linked to a song, for example, 'In and out the dusty bluebells' or 'Oranges and lemons'.

## Top tip

Encourage the children to play cooperatively and to respect each other's comments, ideas and views. Invite parents to help make a decorative plaque or portable stand showing the words 'Friendship stop' for the children to use during daily play sessions.

## Differentiation

Invite older or more confident children to help younger or less confident children to sing the song and join in with the game.

## Further ideas

- Listen to the song 'The Grand Old Duke of York' on the CD-ROM and march around as you sing.
- Ask questions such as, *What is a 'Friendship stop'? What would you do if you saw a child at the 'Friendship stop'?*

# Let's celebrate  It's my party!

**CD-ROM resources**

Which party is the best?

**Early learning goal**

Consider the consequences of their words and actions for themselves and others.

### Setting up

Organise a cosy listening and talking area indoors or outdoors. Listen to the rhyme 'Which party is the best?' on the CD-ROM. Provide a selection of percussion instruments such as bells, tambourines, triangles, drums and shakers.

### Getting started

- Encourage the children to join in saying the rhyme 'Which party is the best?' or singing it to the tune of '1, 2, 3, 4, 5 once I caught a fish alive'. Ask the children to point to a peer as they say the word 'you're'. Explain that saying something kind, such as this, is a compliment. Encourage the children to say something complimentary or kind about others in the group.
- Ask the children to say an adapted version of the rhyme for each child in the group, for example: *Which party is the best? All the parties (Sam's) a guest!* Discuss how kind words make the children feel, for example, happy, pleased and confident.
- Invite the children to repeat the rhymes using a selection of percussion instruments to accompany them.

### Let's talk!

Ask, *Who would you like to say something kind to? What would you say and why?* For children requiring more support, ask *When was the last time someone said something kind to you?* For children requiring challenge, ask *When was the last time you gave a compliment?* Look for children who are willing and able to take turns, share the instruments fairly and join in the music-making activities as part of a group.

### Top tip

Boost self-confidence by inviting individual children to personalise the song, by including the name of a special person, for example: *Which party is the best? All the parties (Gran's) a guest!* Encourage positive relationships by asking the children to share and swap the instruments as they sing.

### Differentiation

Say the rhyme with those who require more support. Challenge those who require further stimulation by inviting them to record their group as they say the rhyme and play the instruments.

### Further ideas

- Provide simple puppets (wooden spoons or strips of card showing a happy face on one side and a sad face on the reverse) and use them for imaginative play, based on parties (attending a party, holding a party, not being invited to a party or not wanting to go to a party).
- Encourage the children to take it in turns to narrate a simple puppet play or invite a group of children to perform their play for an audience such as their peers, parents or siblings.

# Birthdays past and present

## Early learning goal

 Find out about past and present events in their own lives, and in those of their families and other people they know.

## Setting up
Ask parents to help their children collect some old birthday cards sent by friends and family and to tell them about the birthday cards, who they were from and what they did on their special day.

## Getting started
- Invite the children to bring in a selection of old birthday cards and suggest that they use them to make a colourful birthday card collage by cutting out special pictures, messages and numbers printed on the cards to stick randomly over a large blank background.
- During the activity, encourage the children to talk about each card by recalling information told to them at home. Alternatively, ask the children to describe the person who gave them the card or invite them to tell you about happy times they have spent with this person.
- Display the collage on the wall and invite the children to talk to the rest of the group about the pictures, words and numbers they contributed.

## Let's talk!
Ask, *Whose birthday card is this? Was this card sent to a friend or relative?* For children requiring more support, ask *Who gave you this card?* For children requiring challenge, ask, *Did the person who gave you this card have something special to say about their birthday?* Note if the activity has enabled the children to find out about a past event in their own life or in the life of someone they know well.

## Top tip
Prompt less confident speakers by asking 'open' questions about their card selection and by listening to their responses with interest and enthusiasm. Invite parents and grandparents into your setting to help the children create the collage. Alternatively, invite them to view and talk about the collage with their children when it is finished.

## Differentiation
Provide one-to-one assistance during the practical stages such as cutting and gluing for those who require more support. Challenge those who require further stimulation by inviting them to design a decorative border around the collage or to add simple labels, such as 'This was my Nanny's card', 'I gave this card to my uncle', 'Nina saved this card for me'.

## Further ideas
- Look at the photo on the CD-ROM of a child celebrating their first birthday and talk about the scene with the children. Can the children recall early birthdays of their own?
- Ask parents to help the children find out about past events in their own lives, for example, where were they born, when or where did they take their first steps, what was their favourite food, toy or game as a toddler?

# Birthday book

### CD-ROM resources

✏️ Party invitation

Write their own names and other things such as labels and captions, and begin to form simple sentences, sometimes using punctuation.

Work as part of a group or class, taking turns and sharing fairly, understanding that there needs to be agreed values and codes of behaviour for groups of people, including adults and children, to work together harmoniously.

## Setting up

Before the activity, request that parents help their children to collect some photos of their last birthday. Label 12 large sheets of paper with the months of the year. Print a copy of the activity sheet 'Party invitation' (from page 37 or the CD-ROM) for each child.

## Getting started

- Help the children to write their name on their birth month page. Encourage them to work together by decorating the page with photos or drawings about their most recent birthday.
- Scribe simple captions for the children, for example: 'This is me on my 4th birthday' and 'This is me and mummy eating birthday cake'.
- Secure the 12 pages together, between a front and back cover, using a hole punch and ribbon. Help the children to think of a title to write on the front cover, for example, 'Birthday book' or 'We are 4'. Display the book in a prominent position for friends and family to read.

## Let's talk!

Ask, *What date is your birthday? How old will you be on your next birthday?* For children requiring more support, ask *What was your favourite birthday present? Who bought it for you?* For children requiring challenge, ask, *What do you like to do on your birthday?* Notice how confidently the children attempt to write their name.

## Top tip

Use the activity to help boost each child's self-esteem by highlighting the positive contributions they made to the shared 'Birthday book'. Support developing relationships by encouraging the children to interact with one another during the activity and by valuing the contributions of others.

## Differentiation

Provide bold name cards for children to help spell their names. Challenge those who require further stimulation by inviting them to 'write' other words to include in the birthday book.

## Further ideas

- Provide each child with a copy of the activity sheet 'Party invitation' and support them to complete it, for example, 'To White Bear, you are invited to a teddy bears' tea party on Monday from Katie'.
- Encourage the children to use the completed sheets as invitations to a teddy bears' picnic or pretend party in the grounds of your setting.

To _____

**You are invited
to a teddy bears'
tea party**

On _____

From _____

# Favourite festivals

### CD-ROM resources

Patterned streamers

Decorated hands

### Early learning goals

Talk about, recognise and recreate simple patterns.

Use language to imagine and recreate roles and experiences.

## Setting up

View the photo 'Decorated hands' on the CD-ROM showing hands painted with henna ready for a special wedding celebration. Talk about the patterns and ask the children to recall a special event they have attended with family and friends. Encourage them to describe the decorations, special clothing, where they went and how they helped or joined in.

## Getting started

- Provide each child with a printed copy of the activity sheet 'Patterned streamers' from page 39 or print it from the CD-ROM. Invite them to follow the colour code to decorate the shapes on the spiral. Point out the repeated patterns on the spiral and when the pattern changes. Help them to describe one of the repeated patterns, for example, circle, triangle, circle, triangle, or circle, star, circle, star.
- When the children have finished decorating the patterns on the spiral, help them to cut along the dotted lines to create long colourful streamers. Tape a length of thread to the centre of the streamer and show the children how it twists and swirls in the air.
- Hang several streamers, at varying heights, in the home corner or role-play area to create a colourful party scene for imaginative play.

## Let's talk!

Ask, *How many colours are on the streamer? Which shape is pink? How many stars are on the streamer?* For children requiring more support, ask *Can you see a green diamond? What is this shape called?* For children requiring challenge, ask *Are there more circles than stars? How many diamonds can you see? Which shape is in the centre of the spiral?* Note whether the children can talk about the shapes and patterns with confidence. Do they recognise the repeated patterns?

## Top tip

Ensure that every child is involved, for example, supporting children who have physical problems with manipulating tools by offering hand-over-hand support or asking them to identify a sequence for you to colour. Cut out and hang the spiral for them to admire with parents and peers.

## Differentiation

Colour the code along the base of the activity sheet for children requiring more support. Challenge those who require further stimulation by inviting them to adapt the code, for example, stripy red circles or spotty blue triangles.

## Further ideas

- Provide the children with a strip of card to decorate with repeated patterns using coloured paper shapes. Fold and tape the decorated card to create party crowns to wear during role-play.

# Patterned streamers

Follow the code to colour the spiral. Cut along the dotted line to make a streamer.

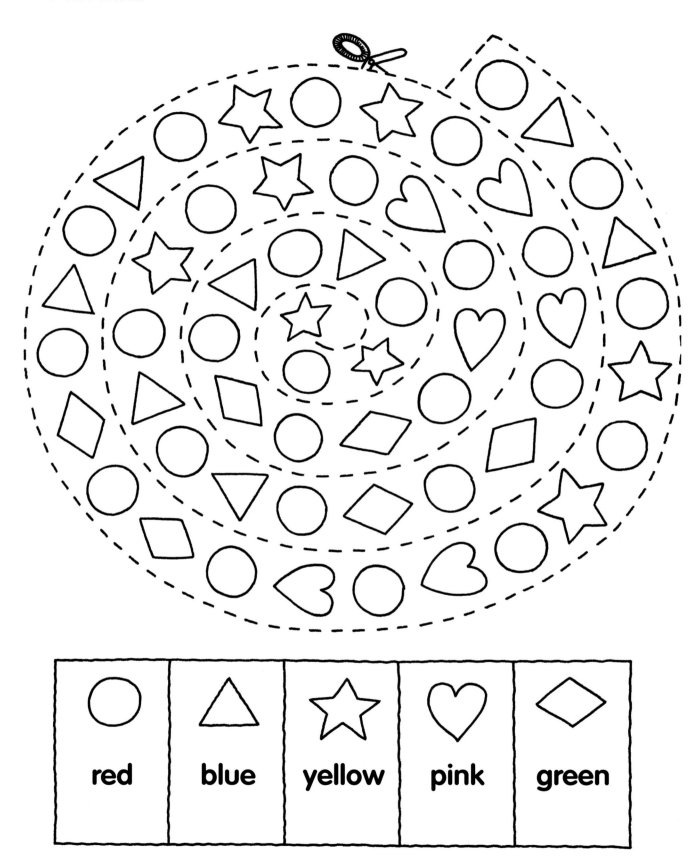

| red | blue | yellow | pink | green |

# Party games

**Early learning goals**

Move with control and coordination.

Recognise and explore how sounds can be changed, sing simple songs from memory, recognise repeated sounds and sound patterns and match movements to music.

## Setting up

Listen to the song 'I am the music man' on the CD-ROM. Provide a selection of percussion instruments that can be played 'on the move', for example, drums with a strap, tambourines, bells, shakers, triangles and wooden blocks.

## Getting started

- Invite the children to listen to the song as they mime the actions of the music man by moving around, avoiding others as they dance, march, skip and weave about the space playing their imaginary instruments.
- Play a game by calling out occasional instructions, for example, *Everybody change direction, March on the spot, Play your instrument up high/down low.*
- Invite the children to select a real percussion instrument. Repeat the game by including instructions such as *Drums only, Bells and triangles together, Play your instrument quietly/loudly* and so on.
- Encourage the children to swap instruments and play again.

## Let's talk!

Encourage the children to imagine and describe what they think the music man looks like. *How does he move? How does he dance? How does he hold his instruments?* For children requiring support, ask *Which instrument did you play?* For children requiring challenge, ask *Can you think of some of the words in the song?* Notice the children's ability to move with control and coordination. Do they have the confidence to create movements to music? Can they join in games that require specific movements?

## Top tip

Make sure that every child is able to join in, for example, support children with walking or movement problems by replacing words such as *dance, skip* and *march* with general terms such as *weave, whiz* and *wander.*

## Differentiation

Provide extra practice time for those who require more support. Challenge those who require further stimulation by asking them to join in singing the words to the song as they play.

## Further ideas

- Provide simple dressing-up clothes such as colourful hats, shirts, cloaks and jackets and invite the children to dress as a colourful party entertainer as they mime the actions of the music man.
- Invite the children to play the interactive game 'Party balloons' on the CD-ROM by clicking on a character to make their balloon pop or float away to reveal a hidden instrument. Can the children identify which instrument each party guest is playing/holding?
- Encourage the children to practise moving with control and avoiding others, for example, walking in a circle, marching up and down, skipping with a partner.

# Celebration cake

### Early learning goals

Use their imagination in art and design, music, dance, imaginative and role-play and stories.

## Setting up
Observe the photo of the celebration cake on the CD-ROM and encourage the children to describe its appearance and to identify what type of celebration it was made for. Talk about the different types of family celebrations that involve a special cake, for example, a birthday, a wedding and a christening. Provide some air-drying clay or salt dough, paints and painting equipment, aprons and hand-washing facilities.

## Getting started
- Invite the children to design and make a pretend celebration cake as a prop for imaginative play using clay or dough. Encourage them to roll, squeeze, coil, press, pat, poke and texture the modelling material using their hands, fingers and simple modelling tools such as shaped cutters, blunt knives and plastic combs.
- When dry, invite the children to paint their model to represent a tasty cake. Talk about the colours they could use and the flavours they represent, for example, brown for chocolate, pink for strawberry flavour, yellow for lemon flavour and so on.
- Invite the children to place the cakes in the role-play area as props for play based on family celebrations, festivals and parties.

## Let's talk!
As the children make the models ask questions such as, *What shape is your cake going to be? What colours will you use to decorate it? Have you ever tasted a real celebration cake?* For children requiring more support, say *Tell me about your cake?* For children requiring a challenge, ask, *How many layers will your cake have? How wide and high will your cake be?* Notice the extent of the children's imagination as they model, paint and play. Do the children require prompting with ideas or do they express ideas with enthusiasm and imagination.

## Top tip
Encourage the children to collaborate with one another, respecting all the models. Encourage the children to invite their parents into the role-play area for a pretend tea party.

## Differentiation
Offer practical help for those who require more support, for example, rolling the clay or dough until soft and pliable, creating textures or mixing paint colours. Challenge those who require further stimulation by inviting them to draw a picture to show the type of the cake they wish to make.

## Further ideas
- Encourage the children to model other types of party food, for example, jam tarts, fairy cakes, dainty sandwiches or specific festival-themed food.
- Invite the children to decorate paper plates, cups and napkins with party designs for use during imaginative play.

## CD-ROM resources

♪ Bobby Shaftoe

### Early learning goals

Understand that people have different needs, views, cultures and beliefs, that need to be treated with respect.

Enjoy listening to and using spoken and written language, and readily turn to it in their play and learning.

ENABLING ENVIRONMENTS

## Setting up

Listen to the song 'Bobby Shaftoe' on the CD-ROM, talk about the words and ask the children to consider why Bobby is so special to someone. Ask the children to consider who is special to them.

## Getting started

- Invite the children to draw or paint a picture of someone who is special to them.
- Help them to write a label or caption for their picture, for example, 'This is my special mummy' or 'I love Auntie Suzie' or 'My grandpa is the best'.
- Hang the pictures and captions in your setting and help the children to write a large title for the display, for example, 'Special person's board', 'Special to me' or 'Very important people'.

## Let's talk!

Encourage the children to listen carefully to the words in the song and ask *Where has Bobby Shaftoe gone? What will Bobby do when he comes back?* For children requiring support, ask *Have you ever waved goodbye to someone when they went away?* For children requiring a challenge, ask *How would you feel if Bobby did not come back?* Notice those children who seem able to understand the feelings of others. Do all the children listen to others with patience and respect? Do they respond to comments with understanding? Do they show empathy?

A UNIQUE CHILD

## Top tip

Help the children to feel confident and proud of their work by involving their parents as much as possible, for example, encourage the children to invite their parents into your setting to view and appreciate the wonderful paintings they have completed as part of themed activities.

POSITIVE RELATIONSHIPS

## Differentiation

Invite those who require more support to bring in a photo of their special person instead of creating a drawing or painting. Challenge those who require further stimulation by inviting them to add a speech bubble to their drawing for you to scribe the words that their special person might say, for example, 'Welcome home', 'I love you', 'How lovely to see you' or 'Come and have some tea my darling'.

## Further ideas

- Invite the children to paint pictures of family members on to giant paper leaves to create a simple family tree.
- Make a 'group tree' with labelled drawings, photos or paintings of staff, helpers, children and pets from your setting. Display the pictures in a prominent position such as the main entrance area. Invite the children to think of a heading for the display, for example, 'Welcome to our group'.

# Special thanks

 **CD-ROM resources**

Girl reading card

**Early learning goal**

Attempt writing for different purposes, using features of different forms such as lists, stories and instructions.

## Setting up

Prepare a folded sheet of card for each child. Provide a wide range of colourful drawing and writing tools, for example, pens, pencils, crayons, pastels, felt-tipped pens and handwriting pens.

## Getting started

- Look at the photo on the CD-ROM of a girl reading a card with the children and talk about what you can see. Discuss why people give and receive cards. Emphasise that one of the reasons is to say 'thank you'.
- Provide the children with a folded sheet of card and invite them to design and decorate a card for someone who deserves a big 'Thank you'. Help the children to write the words 'Thank you' on the inside or outside of the card and to include a simple message to explain why they are saying thank you, for example, 'Thank you for being my friends', 'Thank you for my birthday gifts', 'Thank you for being so kind'.
- Help the children to select or make a simple envelope for their card and invite them to take the card home.

## Let's talk!

Ask, *Why have you decorated your card with this picture? Why have you chosen this person to receive a 'Thank you' card? Do you see this person often?* For children requiring more support, ask *Who is your card for?* For children requiring challenge, ask, *Can you explain why this person deserves to be thanked?* Notice the children who attempt to write their card, even if the activity is new or challenging to them. Are the children willing to write for different purposes, for example, to label the front of the card, to write a simple message inside the card and to write a name on the envelope?

## Top tip

Encourage the children to respect one another's designs and 'thank you' messages by emphasising that every card is special because it has been created with love and care. Support developing relationships by encouraging the children to show an interest in each other's cards by asking questions and by making positive comments.

## Differentiation

Provide individual support for those who require extra help. Challenge those who seek further stimulation by asking them to fulfil the writing strategies employed in your setting to their very best ability, for example, to form each letter correctly or to write everything independently.

## Further ideas

- Invite the children to use finger paints to write messages on a giant-sized card.
- Encourage the children to write 'thank you' notes to helpers in your setting such as the cleaner, the lunch time supervisors and the secretary.

# Your own special way

### Early learning goals

Sustain attentive listening, responding to what they have heard with relevant comments, questions or actions.

Be confident to try new activities, initiate ideas and speak in a familiar group.

### Setting up

Look at the photo on the CD-ROM of the girl riding her bicycle and talk about the scene with the children. Make a card photocopy of the activity sheet on page 45 'Achievement badges' for each child or print it from the CD-ROM.

### Getting started

- Encourage the children to reflect on their personal achievements, for example, learning to ride a bicycle, gaining the confidence to join a club and so on.
- Provide each child with a printed copy of the activity sheet 'Achievement badges' and invite them to colour in and cut out the 'Well Done' badge at the top of the sheet and to present it to a partner in the group saying why that person deserves the badge. Ensure that everybody in the group receives a badge.
- Next, invite the children to decorate the blank badge for themselves by writing and drawing about a second achievement they are particularly proud of, and to add words or pictures. Help the children to cut out the second badge to wear and use Velcro to secure the badges to their clothing.
- Use the activity to help explain that everybody is special in their own way.

### Let's talk!

Ask, *What are your badges for? Who did you give a badge to and why?* For children requiring more support, ask *What are you proud of doing?* For children requiring challenge, ask *What did you find difficult?* Notice those children who have gained the skill of attentive listening. Do all the children respond to what they have heard with relevant comments, questions or actions?

### Top tip

Make sure that every child has two badges to wear, for example, support children with physical problems by offering 'hand-over-hand' assistance or by asking them to provide verbal instructions as you decorate the badge for them. Develop positive relationships by encouraging the children to talk to one another about their badges and to praise each other's achievements.

### Differentiation

Cut out the badges in advance for those who require more support. Challenge those who require further stimulation by inviting them to talk to adults, at home or in your setting, about the things they are proud of. Invite the children to design a suitable badge, or certificate, to present to an adult of their choice.

### Further ideas

- Help the children to find out about people in your locality who have achieved something good for their community or whose job involves helping others, for example, firefighters and ambulance crew.

**Design a badge for yourself.**

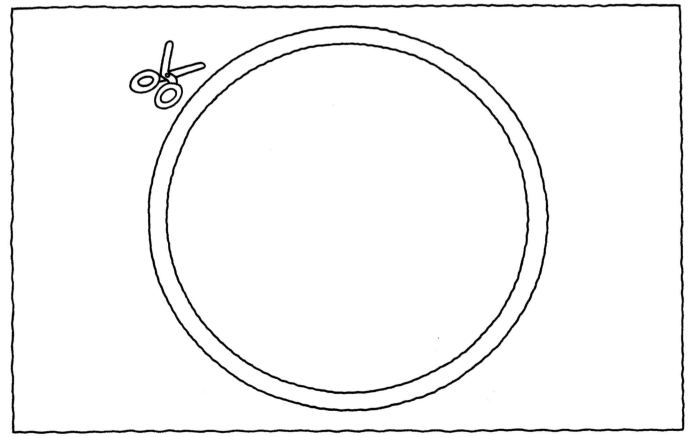

# Special people in special places

**Early learning goal**

Observe, find out about and identify features in the place they live and the natural world.

### Setting up.

Observe the photo on the CD-ROM of a family having a picnic and talk about the scene with the children. Ask, *Where is your favourite place for a family outing? Are this family in the countryside or in a busy town?*

### Getting started

- Go on a walk or look at photos of familiar buildings or places of natural beauty locally. Talk about happy places, for example, buildings or houses where the children have had happy times. *Why do the places seem happy?* Because of the people inside the building!
- Invite the children to paint a picture or take a photo of a building or place that holds a happy memory.
- If possible, ask parents to become involved in the activity by helping their children to draw, paint or photograph a building or scene, outside the locality, that holds a special place in their heart.
- Invite the children to display their pictures on the wall or in a large book and help them to label them with words, captions or sentences explaining why the places are so special to them.

### Let's talk!

Ask, *Why is this a happy place to be? Who lives in this house and why do they make the place seem special?* For children requiring more support, ask *Can you show me a picture of your happy place?* For children requiring challenge, ask *Where do you feel happiest and why?* Notice those children who are keen to observe, describe and find out about the place they live and the natural world.

### Top tip

During discussions make sure that everyone is aware that their comments and responses are respected and valued by you and the rest of the group. Involve parents during this activity, for example, by sharing local knowledge, by joining in a local walk and by helping the children to take, print and sort photos.

### Differentiation

Work on a one-to-one basis with those who require more support. Challenge those who require further stimulation by inviting them to use a digital camera to take photos of their special place. Help them to use a computer to print the image or to make changes using functions such as crop, resize and rename.

### Further ideas

- Ask parents to help the children record the sounds of their special place, (children playing in the park, ducks quacking on the pond) and bring them in to share with the group.
- Observe features, buildings and places of worship relevant to all the children in the local community and talk about the positive contributions made by all cultures.

# A special gift

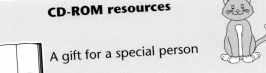

**Early learning goal**

Handle tools, objects, construction and malleable materials safely and with increasing control.

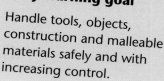

## Setting up
Encourage the children to help collect a wide range of tools and recycled and decorative materials for a craft activity. Listen to the story 'A gift for a special person' on the CD-ROM and explain that making a gift for someone means it is unique and special because you have to put thought and effort into it.

## Getting started
- Invite the children to make a unique gift for someone special using recycled and decorative materials. Talk about who the children will make a gift for and encourage them to select a simple and relevant theme for the gift, for example, a younger sibling might enjoy a homemade toy or mobile, a relative or friend who is a long way away might like a picture or collage sent through the post.
- Invite the children to explore the range of materials on offer. Encourage them to consider how they could trim, cut, shape and decorate the materials to create something interesting and 'new'. Invite the children to experiment by trying out several different ideas, adapting their work and reselecting tools or materials used.
- Encourage the children to discover which ideas are the most successful via trial and error. Emphasise that mistakes do not matter: if something does not turn out right, encourage the children to try again!
- When complete, invite the children to design and make a personalised gift tag to attach to the gift.

## Let's talk!
Ask, *Who are you making a gift for? What ideas have you tried so far?* For children requiring more support, ask *Do you enjoy making presents?* For children requiring challenge, ask *Can you think of a message to write on the gift tag?* Notice those children who are willing and able to handle tools, objects, construction and malleable materials safely and with increasing control.

## Top tip
Encourage the children to collaborate with one another, respecting all the models and constructions. Invite parents in to view an exhibition of the special gifts before they are given away by the children.

## Differentiation
Help build the confidence of those who require more support. Challenge those who require further stimulation by inviting them to prepare and tidy up after the activity.

## Further ideas
- Encourage the children to retell the story on the CD-ROM in their own words.
- If children wish to make a gift for a baby or toddler help them to create something safe for a young child to hold or suggest ideas such as a name plaque for their door.

# I am special

**CD-ROM resources**

Ten special children

Ten happy children

**Early learning goal**

Explore colour, texture, shape, form and space in two or three dimensions.

## Setting up

Listen to the song on the CD-ROM 'Ten special children' and encourage the children to mime actions as they sing the song, to the tune of 'There were ten in the bed'. Pause after *We'll show you* each time while the children dance, skip, mime or move in their own way. Continue singing until *Now it's time for one to go* and pause again while one child makes a dramatic exit. Continue until the final verse and invite the last child to sing, *I am one special child, with lots of special friends, good-bye, good-bye* and ask all the children to return to bow or wave good-bye.

## Getting started

- Provide a group of children with a large sheet of paper to share and a selection of paints and painting equipment. Encourage the children to work as a team by decorating the large sheet of paper with pictures of ten children showing off their special talents.

- Emphasise that all painting styles and abilities are welcome! Invite the children to frame the painting or to fill the gaps with ten pairs of handprints and ten child signatures. Display the giant poster on the wall with a printed copy of the rhyme.

## Let's talk!

Ask, *What is your special talent? Can you remember the words to the rhyme?* For children requiring more support, ask *Which picture did you paint on the poster?* For children requiring challenge, ask *Can you think of a title for the poster?* Notice those children who are interested in using a variety of colour to create images. Are the children beginning to gain an awareness of shape and form? Are they willing and able to share an area of paper with their peers by using the space fairly and imaginatively?

## Top tip

Boost self-esteem and confidence by encouraging the children to talk about, paint a picture, or to bring in a photo of themselves displaying their special talent. Emphasise that a special talent is as unique as each individual. Invite the children to stage a performance of the song and mime for parents.

## Differentiation

Provide a range of brushes or finger-paints for those who require more support. Challenge those who require further stimulation by inviting them to mix their own colours or to add details such as patterns on the clothing, bows in hair and expressions on the children's faces.

## Further ideas

- Invite the children to join in the interactive game 'Ten happy children' on the CD-ROM by clicking on the characters to make them wave and jump up and down in numerical order.